WILD, WILD WORDS ACTIVITY BOOK

by Gabriella DeGennaro
illustrated by Scott Brooks

FIND PHIL AND PHYLLIS!

Are you feeling wild? So are Phil and Phyllis! Count the number of times they appear on the activity pages of this book.

Write your answer here: _____

MAD LIBS
An imprint of Penguin Random House LLC, New York

First published in the United States of America by Mad Libs,
an imprint of Penguin Random House LLC, New York, 2023

Mad Libs format and text copyright © 2023 by Penguin Random House LLC

Concept created by Roger Price & Leonard Stern

Designed by Dinardo Design

Visit us online at penguinrandomhouse.com.

Manufactured in China

ISBN 9780593523223

1 3 5 7 9 10 8 6 4 2

HH

RIDICULOUSLY SIMPLE INSTRUCTIONS

Mad Libs is an amazing way to create your own hysterically funny stories! To play, fill in the blanks with different types of words, like nouns, adjectives, or even exclamations. In case you've forgotten what nouns, adjectives, verbs, and adverbs are, here is a quick review:

A **NOUN** is the name of a person, place, or thing. *Toaster, umbrella, bathtub,* and *pillow* are nouns. A Mad Libs will sometimes ask for a specific type of noun, like an **ANIMAL** (*tiger*), **ARTICLE OF CLOTHING** (*glove*), **OCCUPATION** (*astronaut*), or **CELEBRITY** (*Abraham Lincoln*). When a Mad Libs asks for **A PLACE**, it means any location (*Africa, barbershop, kitchen,* or *coral reef*).

An **ADJECTIVE** describes something or someone. *Lumpy, soft, pretty, messy,* and *tall* are adjectives. A Mad Libs will sometimes ask for a specific type of adjective, like a **COLOR** (*blue*).

A **VERB** is an action word. *Eat, sculpt,* and *collect* are verbs. A Mad Libs will sometimes ask for a **VERB ENDING IN "S"** (*runs*), a **VERB ENDING IN "ING"** (*pitching*), or a **VERB (PAST TENSE)** (*jumped* or *swam*).

An **ADVERB** tells how something is done. It modifies a verb and usually ends in "ly." *Quickly, wildly,* and *carefully* are adverbs.

An **EXCLAMATION** is anything a person or other creature would say, like *hey!, wow!, ouch!, meow!,* or *yikes!* **A SILLY WORD** is any made-up word or a word that just sounds funny, like *ooopatoopa!, squipple!,* or *whammo!* **A SOUND** is any noise, like *boing!, ding!, grunt!,* or *screech!*

When a Mad Libs asks for a **PLURAL**, it means more than one. For example, the plural of *cat* is *cats.*

When a Mad Libs asks for the **SAME** type of word, write in the same word you chose earlier in the story. For example, if you chose *chair* as a **NOUN** earlier in the story, you would write *chair* again for the **SAME NOUN**.

Feel the Heat!

Whew! It's hot, and these tall giraffes need some shade from the sun. On the branches below, write six nouns that start with the letter G. Then count the number of letters in each word and add them together to get your score! Use the score key to see how many stickers from the back of the book you can put on this page. Help those giraffes find some shade! Add sunglasses and hats if you want! Get wild!

SCORE: _____

SCORE KEY:
30+: 30 stickers
25–29: 25 stickers
20–24: 20 stickers
15–19: 15 stickers
0–14: 10 stickers

Beware of the ...?

_____ ! I can't believe my _____ !
EXCLAMATION   PART OF THE BODY (PLURAL)

Watch out! You've just discovered a totally new wild animal hiding in the jungle. Complete this Mad Libs to name your creature and describe its features!

Scientific Name: _____ -idon _____ -icus maximus
                        PERSON IN ROOM   A PLACE

Description: Head of a/an _____ + tail of a/an _____ + body
                                  ANIMAL   ANIMAL

of a/an _____
            ANIMAL

Creature Features

_____ whiskers
    ADJECTIVE

Large _____
        PART OF THE BODY (PLURAL)

_____ fur with a/an _____ -shaped pattern
    COLOR   NOUN

_____ _____ teeth
    NUMBER   ADJECTIVE

Three _____
        PART OF THE BODY (PLURAL)

_____ feet with sharp _____
    ADJECTIVE   PLURAL NOUN

Country of origin: _____
                          COUNTRY

Favorite food: _____ with _____ on top
                      TYPE OF FOOD   SOMETHING ALIVE

Personality: _____ and _____
                    ADJECTIVE   ADJECTIVE

Intelligence: Smarter than the average _____
                                              NOUN

Draw your creature here!

Connect the Cubs

Oh no! These cubs got separated from their mamas!

To solve the puzzle, draw a line from each mama to her cub by looking for the leopard with the same spots!

Name That Leopard!

Aww! These cute cubs need cute names!
Can you find and circle all the adorable
cub names in this word search?

```
T  L  C  U  D  K  I  S  S  E  S  L  A  D  C  S  M
U  U  S  Q  U  E  I  K  M  D  F  M  U  S  U  W  Y
G  C  U  D  D  L  E  B  O  O  A  B  Y  D  T  E  L
P  F  I  S  H  Y  N  T  O  U  L  H  O  R  I  E  B
Y  Q  K  Y  T  B  U  O  C  N  O  O  D  L  E  T  Y
R  O  A  R  Y  I  L  E  H  Z  S  N  P  Y  P  U  H
M  T  V  W  S  T  L  T  E  B  A  E  B  E  I  M  N
P  F  M  I  S  T  Y  T  S  U  L  Y  O  R  E  S  B
Y  Q  U  Y  T  Y  U  O  C  Z  H  M  U  F  F  I  N
V  W  S  I  N  B  B  A  B  Y  D  O  L  L  K  L  F
M  T  H  W  S  A  L  T  H  B  A  S  B  E  J  K  V
P  F  Q  S  H  B  N  T  O  U  L  R  O  R  P  C  B
I  K  I  T  T  Y  C  A  K  E  S  E  R  Z  A  L  C
V  Y  K  A  R  L  I  E  N  M  U  S  X  T  G  F  S
```

BABYDOLL
BITTYBABY
CUDDLEBOO
CUTIEPIE
SWEETUMS

ROARY
KARL
KISSES
KITTYCAKES
MUFFIN

MUSH
NOODLE
HONEY
SMOOCHES
MISTY

Those names are so

_____ !
ADJECTIVE

Spelling Bee

Can you spot the spelling mistake in each of the words below?
Find and circle the letters that don't belong,
and use them to spell out the punch line to this joke:

What kind of bug works at the bank?

A __ __ __ __ __ __   __ __ __!

termmite	crincket	beeytle	tarantuela
cicadoa	monarche butterfly	bearwig	mosqueito

Bug Picnic!

Bugs love a good picnic!
Use the stickers in the back of this book to create the biggest bug picnic ever!

Eye'm Watching You

_____! Use the **Parts of Speech Key** to color
EXCLAMATION

in the picture and reveal the answer to the question below.

Fuzzy

Busy

Hungrily

Quickly

Tiny

Buzzed

Weird

Squeezed

Creepy

Nice

Ants

Grew

Flipped

Hairy

Odd

Noisily

Colony

Perfectly

Tree

Cute

Wildly

Gross

Feet

Screamed

Stomped

Flea

Wasps

Honey

Slithered

Insects

Slimy

Strange

Bee

Slowly

Petals

Sky

Spiders

Flew

Roared

Dirt

Stinger

Gnats

Stung

Bashfully

Suddenly

Scary

Flowers

Amazing

Silly

Eat

How many eyes do caterpillars have? _____

9

Walk on the Wild Side!

Yikes! Phil is walking way more letters than he can handle! Trace Phil's leashes to find the letters that spell out the name of his mystery pet.

Phil's mystery pet is a __ __ __ __ __ __ __ .

Polar Pen Pals!

Patricia Penguin and Peter Polar Bear have been pen pals for years! Complete Patricia's letter to her Polar Bear Bestie!

Dear Peter Polar Bear,

How are things up at the North _____ ? I've got some _____
                                                     NOUN   ADJECTIVE

news from down here in (the) _____ . A film crew just set up
                                         A PLACE

a film _____ on my iceberg! They're here to _____
            TYPE OF BUILDING   VERB

and observe _____ like me for a/an _____ nature
              ANIMAL (PLURAL)   ADJECTIVE

documentary. That means I might be the next Hollywood _____ ! My
                                                        NOUN

black-and- _____ _____ was made for the movie screen!
                COLOR   PART OF THE BODY

I could be the next _____ ! I just have to impress the film's famous
                         CELEBRITY

_____ with my _____ looks and _____ swim
      OCCUPATION   ADJECTIVE   ADJECTIVE

moves. I'll _____ schools of fish to show off, too! Anchovies may not be
           VERB

_____ , but they are delicious. Do you think I can eat _____
    ADJECTIVE   NUMBER

pounds of fish without getting a/an _____ -ache? I'd do anything it takes
                                   PART OF THE BODY

for my _____ minutes of fame!
         NUMBER

Your almost-famous _____ ,
                       NOUN

Patricia Penguin

Use the stickers in the back of this book to create Patricia Penguin's very first movie poster here:

MOVIE TITLE

Opposite Otters!

Sometimes opposites attract! Each of the otters on the left has a best friend on the right who is their total opposite. But what does their opposite otter look like?

For each otter on the right, fill in the words that are the opposite of the words under the otters on the left. Draw the opposite otters and use the stickers in the back of this book to help fill in what they look like!

Otter 1

Frowning   Short-haired   Shy

Opposite Otter 1

_____   _____   _____

Otter 2

Old   Cute   Small fangs

Opposite Otter 2

_____   _____   _____

Clowning Around

Clown fish are the comedians of the sea.
Complete their jokes to prove it:

What's a/an _____ duck's favorite snack?
ADJECTIVE

Cheese and *quackers*.

What did the lion say to the _____?
ANIMAL

Pleased to *eat* you.

What kind of underwater _____ can you see in the dark?
NOUN

A *star*fish!

What do you call a cow who gets a brand-new _____ for their birthday?
VEHICLE

Spoiled milk.

What did the horse say after falling down?

_____! I've fallen and I can't *giddy*-up!
EXCLAMATION

Why didn't the _____ want to play cards with the jungle cat?
ANIMAL

Because she was a *cheetah*!

What do you call an alligator with a magnifying _____?
NOUN

An investi*gator*!

Answer Key

Page 1

Phil and Phyllis appear **12** times on the activity pages of this book. They are on pages 3, 4, 5, 6, 7, 8, 10, 12, 13, 14, and 15.

Page 6

Page 7

Page 8

The answer is "A money bee!" termmite, cicadoa, crincket, monarche butterfly, beeytle, bearwig, tarantuela, mosqueito

Page 9

Caterpillars have **12** eyes.

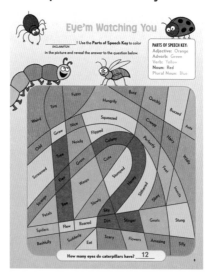

Pages 10–11

Phil's mystery pet is a parrot.

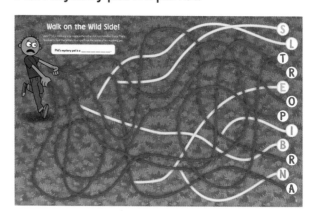